The Eye of the Beholder:

A Dominican's perspective of Cultural

Dualism on the Island of Hispaniola

By
Carlos Ariel Then

COPYRIGHT

<u>Introduction</u>

What does it mean to be beautiful?

Have you ever looked in the mirror and questioned what it is that you like or dislike about yourself? It seems as though we are constantly battling these questions. Look at a map of the Caribbean and you'll find a relatively small island by the name of "Hispaniola", which is separated into two countries. You may not even know what these two countries are because the differences between them are so vast. Despite these differences, they exist, sharing one piece of land which is naturally surrounded by water.

"There is only one other island that shares a similar circumstance" called

St. Martin, which is French speaking on one side, and Dutch on the other (Cambeira 20). The left side of Hispaniola holds a country by the name of Haiti, which speaks French as their national language, and Creole as a secondary. To the right side of the island lies Dominican Republic, a Spanish speaking country. One may compare these two countries to fraternal twins which look nothing alike. Although these two countries share the island of Hispaniola, a different approach to colonization has caused cultural dualism and a divide between the two that delves deeper than many other feuding nations in the world; disdain has become evident and a pervasive racism centered on ancestry continues to promote conflict between the two.

<u>Breaking Free of Haiti</u>

"The Dominican Republic, which came into being an independent nation-state in 1844 by delinking from Haiti, which had unified the island under its rule 22 years earlier, broke the pattern of typical independence movements in its region." Rather than separating itself from its original European colonial powers, the Dominican Republic gained its freedom by dissolving itself from a former colony, a nation founded by ex-slaves (Howard preface 9). At

first things were not so controversial

between the two nations. Juan Pablo

Duarte, the architect of sorts of the new

republic posited the vision of a

multiracial society, and stirred up the

region going so far as to abolish slavery

"forever". To push things further, it

was said that "Slaves coming from

abroad would automatically be set free

upon setting foot on Dominican Soil"

(Howard preface 10). It was also said

that Haitians on the Dominican side of the Island had no fear of expulsion or physical harm. What makes things more radical is that slavery still existed in Puerto Rico until 1878 and in Cuba until 1886; therefore, there was an influx of runaway slaves trying to make it to the Dominican Republic, from surrounding islands.

Underlying Anti-Haitianism

Duarte seemed to be on the verge of establishing an anti-racist society, but something went wrong; perhaps the underlying racism towards their oppressors, and the "undisputed accord of the nation which was no volver al dominio haitiano" or "to not return to Haitian domination" (Cambeira pg.153). Could this be what caused a strong distinction between both countries? Another notable event which caused a greater divide between the two countries was the ludicrous rule of President Trujillo, who implemented an era of "anti-haitianism" which involved

exuberant amounts of bloodshed for the

entire Island.

<u>A Terrible Benefactor of the Land</u>

"Throughout the era of Trujillo,

the Dominican and Haitian people

survived a period of unprecedented

tyranny. It is said that perhaps no other

Latin American ruler presented a more

spectacular record of actual material

achievement in the form of impressive

buildings and massive public works, or

a more heinous record of reprehensible human rights atrocities." (Cambeira 12). This sycophantic man raised thousands of monuments of himself in the capital city of Santo Domingo, which he thought fit to rename "Ciudad Trujillo", and even went so far as to have churches hang up signs that said "Dios en cielo, Trujillo en tierra" which translates to "God in Heaven, Trujillo on Earth". He openly accepted Jews and Spanish immigrants to wash out the "darkness" within the country, and massacred "18,000 Haitians and dark-skinned Dominicans" (Howard 157) during the Parsley Massacre of 1937. This genocide was given its named based on the idea that soldiers went around asking people to pronounce the word parsley. Incorrect pronunciation resulted in death.

<u>Death by Pronunciation</u>

This phenomenon was described as

"Being killed in the night because they

couldn't manage to trill their 'r' or utter

a throaty 'j' to ask for parsley"

(Matibag 147). You see, the word

parsley is pronounced "perejil" in

Spanish; however, it is pronounced

differently in French or Creole than it is

in Spanish. Trujillo's hate towards

Haitians and those with darker skin was

so passionate, it allowed for something

so simple as pronunciation to determine their fate. The languages spoken between the two countries are certainly different, and can be traced back to the original colonizers of each respective country.

Some light on the Dark Side

Haiti was originally colonized by the Spanish who set sail with Christopher Columbus to discover new land. Mass influxes of African slaves were transferred over after much of the indigenous population was wiped out due to massacre, and newly transferred diseases. Most of the indigenous people, known as the Taïno and Arawak Indians, were massacred due to their physical inability to carry out the hard labor which was demanded by their colonizer, who tried to enslave them. In efforts to increase production, stronger slaves were brought in from Africa, commencing the darker skinned population of the Haitian people. The

French took over the island soon after, leaving the Spanish colonizers to focus on the other half of the island. The same occurred on the Dominican side of the Island; however, many of the Spanish colonizers took to mating with the indigenous women and African slaves, which created a more mulatto society. Why did each country develop in such a way? "Haiti and the Dominican Republic- Roots of division" (Youtube). A documentary by

PBS tells us that the relationship between slave and master on the Dominican side of the island became much friendlier once slavery transitioned from sugar cane plantations to a more cattle ranch focused approach. Master and slave relations became very different when compared to the rest of the Caribbean, which perhaps explains their love for their colonizers.

<u>Pulling at the Roots</u>

While the Dominican side of the Island held on tightly to its European roots and religion, and had many of its colonizers leave freely after the sugar cane industry collapsed. The Haitian side of the Island eventually gained its independence from France in 1804, resulting in Haiti being the first black republic. They outnumbered the French colonizers 10 to 1, and revolted.

Because so many new shipments of

slaves had arrived, that side of the island maintained much of its African roots, culture, and religion. Like the Dominican Republic however this country experiences many traumatizing political leaders. Most notable was the Duvalier Regime when corrupt dictator Francois Duvalier, also known as "Papa Doc" like Trujillo, accounted for thousands of deaths. Voodoo, a religion brought over by the African slaves, was a major aspect of Haitian culture, and

Duvalier used this to keep the head of his opponent who tried to overthrow him. He even went as far as referring to himself as a "Loa", a voodoo spirit, to illustrate the power which he had over his people.

Looking in the Mirror

Interestingly, although these two countries started off as colonies, and their population are majorly mulatto or black, the Dominican Republic looks to Spain as their motherland rather than

Africa, despite the fact that hardly any Spanish traits can be seen in the mirror. Contrary to the Dominican Republic, Haiti ensures to educate everyone on the country's history, stressing the importance of African roots. Dominicans have a hard time identifying themselves as "black" and most even find it insulting. Haitian's are proud to be a nation which houses people of all shades, whether they are black, mulatto, or even diaspora.

Haitians take so much pride in their culture; they may even grow offended if they are mistaken as something else which does not celebrate their roots.

The Disparity of it All

This leads to the next question as to why there is such disparity in two races that seem to come from the same roots. A major to this is the "superiority complex" that Dominicans have over Haitians, which comes from Haitian migrant workers doing jobs in The

Dominican Republic that no Dominican would do. A condition of total destitution for the Haitians provided Dominicans with a racist ideology that to this day warps the minds of those who live on the Island of Hispaniola.

One Step Forward, Two Steps Back

Recently, The Dominican Republic was one of the first responders to aid Haiti after the 7.0 magnitude earthquake that rocked the country in 2010. "But the goodwill seems to have dissipated and old tensions resurfaced. Just recently

the Dominican Republic's highest court

ruled to revoke the citizenship of

children of illegal Haitian migrant

workers – a measure to be applied to

anyone born after 1929, and thus

affecting not only migrants' children,

but their grandchildren and, in some

cases, even great-grandchildren."

(Gibson). Conflict still stirs between

the two, even after such a tragic event.

In "1960 both the Dominican Republic

and Haiti had the same per capita real

GDP of US$800. But by 2005

Dominican Republic's per capita real

GDP had tripled to about US$2500,

whereas that of Haiti had halved to

US$430. (Jaramillo, Sancak 4). The

two countries also sit on different ends

of the spectrum as far as average

annual GDP growths are concerned in

the entire Caribbean and Latin

America. (Figure 1).

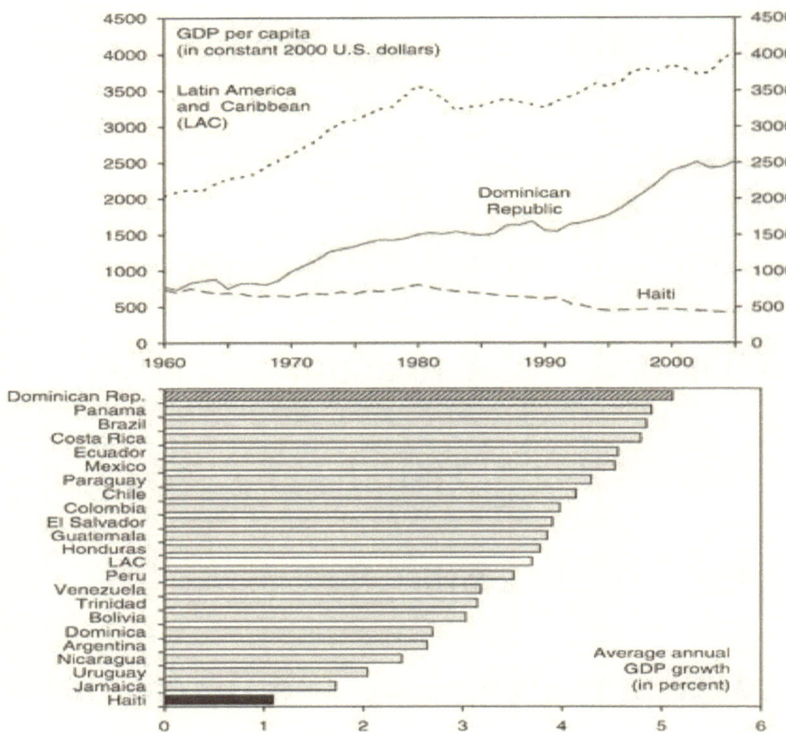

<u>Why's the Grass is Greener?</u>

One of the main contributors to

this major growth is the increase in

tourism, which has successfully

pumped money into the Dominican

economy, rapidly developing the

country as a whole, over the course of

20 years. With many resorts and hotels

established to highlight much of the

natural beauty of the Dominican

Republic, many tourists have flocked to

the country for vacations. This has also

resulted in many foreigners both

investing in businesses within the

country, and also settling there as well.

Unfortunately, Haiti has not

experienced the same luck with their

tourism industry. Lack of government correlation with foreign investors and donors has caused many development projects to either be cancelled, or abandoned mid process. In many ways, this has caused regression rather than progression on Haiti's part. Stephanie Villedroin, the current minister of tourism in Haiti, who also happened to be a descendant of mulatto ancestors, has launched an intense campaign to adopt the model of the Dominican

Republic, as well as many other neighboring countries and islands, to use tourism as an outlet for developing the country. She has gone as far as rejuvenating Haitian nightlife, and highlighting many of Haiti's cultural riches such as their restaurants, beaches, waterfalls, caves, mountains, and many other attractions as well. Only time will tell whether or not this campaign will be a success, or a hindrance to the country's development, thus far, positive results have been assumed.

<u>Beautiful, are they?</u>

With regards to these two countries, we can see a clear situation where cultural pride and history play a major role in keeping these two countries from joining together as one, and being a powerhouse, which benefits from the resources of one another. The way in which the two countries came to fruition leaves an underlying bad taste of one another that may never be

replaced by something tasteful. If you

speak to a Haitian, they will

passionately speak to you about the

beauty, which they see in their country.

"Ayïti Cheri" is a common way which

Haitians refer to their country, which

translates to "Haiti, my love". It is as

though they have personified their

country, giving it romantic features of a

perfect lover. In their eyes, their

country is still the "Pearl of the

Antilles", a nickname which was given

to the country due to its natural beauty.

In the same sense, Dominicans exude

extreme pride in their country, which

has undeniably resulted in their

superiority complex over Haitians.

Dominicans, like the Haitians, pride

themselves in their historical past, their

socially accepted appearance, as well as

their vast development when compared

to their sister country. With beauty

being in the eye of the beholder each

country has beheld their own beauty

through their own eyes, rather than

looking at one another through the eyes

of a kaleidoscope; which would allow

them to see the amazingly numerous

beauties that are housed by each.

<u>Conclusion</u>

So, disdain is still very evident

amongst the two countries. An

underlying pervasive racism centered

on ancestry continues to promote

conflict between the two and even after

all this time the two sister countries have never once held hands. If you recall, at one point these two countries had the same GDP and could be considered equals. Since then one has moved upward while the other has done the complete opposite. This in my opinion is due to the way in which colonialism has impacted each part of the Island of Hispaniola causing cultural dualism between the two inhabiting countries. On the Eastern side Colonists were harsh,

outnumbered, and not unlike what one

would imagine a slave/master

relationship to be. On the Western side,

slavery took a different path and

masters and slaves rode horses and held

machetes. This harsh mistreatment led

the Haitians to revolt and obtain their

freedom and drive out the French and

Spanish, and also "liberate" their sister

country becoming the first Black

Republic. But this did not bode well for

the Western side which was taken from what they might have considered to be "good" hands and placed under control of hands that seemed much more "savage". It's difficult to say if the two countries will ever truly get over what has happened in the past, after all it is what has shaped them. But maybe if each were to take a moment to not just believe that they are beautiful, but actually take a moment to look at themselves in the "mirror" and reflect on themselves as a country, maybe some progress can be made. If these two countries were to work together to attract tourism to the Island of Hispaniola and exploit all of it's natural beauty rather than just half I believe that it will prosper. Beauty may be in the eye of the beholder, but there's only some parts of each country that are truly beautiful when compared to the entire Island.

Works Cited

- Cambeira, Alan. *Quisqueya La Bella: The Dominican Republic in Historical and Cultural Perspective*. 1st ed. N.p.: M E Sharpe, 1996. Print. Perspectives on Latin America and the Caribbean.

- "FIGURE 1." *IMF Staff Papers*. N.p., n.d. Web. 14 Apr. 2014.

- Gibson, Carrie. "The Dominican Republic and Haiti: One Island Riven by an Unresolved past." *Theguardian.com*. Guardian News and Media, 07 Oct. 2013. Web. 14 Apr. 2014.

- "Haiti and The Dominican Republic - The Roots of Division (Massacre River)." *YouTube*. YouTube, 12 Oct. 2012. Web. 14 Apr. 2014.

- Howard, David John. *Coloring the Nation: Race and Ethnicity in the Dominican Republic*. Oxford, U.K.: Signal, 2001. Print.

- Jaramillo, Laura, and Cemile Sancak. "Why Has the Grass Been Greener on One Side of Hispaniola? A Comparative Growth Analysis of the Dominican Republic and

Haiti." *IMF Staff Papers* 56.2 (2009): 323-49. Print.

- Matibag, Eugenio. *Haitian-Dominican Counterpoint: Nation, State, and Race on Hispaniola*. New York: Palgrave, 2003. Print.

- "Rafael Trujillo." *Wikipedia*. Wikimedia Foundation, 14 Apr. 2014. Web. 14 Apr. 2014.